Arthur J. Lembo, Jr.
2015

Copyright © 2015 by Arthur J. Lembo, Jr.

All rights reserved. This book or any portion thereof may not be reproduced or used in any manner whatsoever without the express written permission of the author except for the use of brief quotations in a book review or scholarly journal.

First Printing: July, 2015

Arthur J. Lembo, Jr.
1440 East Sandy Acres Drive
Salisbury, MD 21804

www.artlembo.wordpress.com

Preface

In 2004, I created a small publication with my students titled *How Do I Do that In ArcGIS/Manifold*. It was an enormously fun endeavor, which to my surprise really took off in the GIS community. There were tens of thousands of downloads, some lengthy debate, and finally some attempts to replicate the document for other GIS software products. Seeing the document take on a life of its own was really gratifying. This current document is a continuation of that theme, but with a focus on the use of spatial SQL in PostGIS to accomplish the tasks.

Once again, we will revisit the 1988 United States Geological Survey (USGS) classic document titled *The Process for Selecting Geographic Information Systems*[1] (Guptil, et. al., 1988). As you might recall from the previous *How Do I Do That* document, the USGS report provided an overview of the process for selecting geographic information systems, in addition to a checklist of functions that a GIS should include. The functions were broken into five separate categories: user interface, database management, database creation, data manipulation and analysis, and data display and presentation.

This book is the second of three publications on how to perform the USGS tasks using the SQL syntax in PostGIS. While this book illustrates the GIS processes allowable in PostGIS 2.0, the other books will include a discussion of Manifold GIS SQL, and potentially the new software under development by Manifold Software, Ltd. (currently named Radian).

As the title indicates, I envision this book to act as a sort of reference to the question of *how do I do that..*, residing on the user's lap while attempting to implement GIS functionality with PostGIS SQL. Also, I believe simply perusing through the pages will be convincing enough to cause users to consider the use of SQL as part of their daily GIS activities. As a teaching tool, one can see how many of the same SQL functions are just reused in a different fashion to complete a task, without the need to run some kind of special wizard or new tool. So, if you can write SQL, you can build all kinds of functionality in GIS.

You will also notice that this book is much shorter than the original *How do I do that in ArcGIS/Manifold*, and without illustrations. This was done on purpose to keep the cost of production low and to allow users to quickly get an answer to their spatial SQL questions. Many excellent books on PostGIS and PostGRES already exist, and you can consult them when you have mastered these topics. However, I believe that users will continue to make use of this book to accomplish the tasks in SQL. Finally, all of the examples were tested using PostGIS 2.0 with PostGRES 9.3. A dump of that database is downloadable from my blog:

---

[1] Guptill, S., D. Cotter, R. Gibson, R. Liston, H. Tom, T. Trainer, H. VanWyhe. 1988. "A Process for Selecting Geographic Information Systems". Technology Working Group – Technical Report 1. USGS Open File Report 88-105.

artlembo.wordpress.com. Therefore, users can recreate the SQL in the book on the actual data. To do that of course, the queries in this book must be retyped. This too was done on purpose - retyping the queries are the best way to learn. Simply copying and pasting the queries is not going to help you learn what is actually happening. So, while there is a little more effort on the part of the reader, I believe it will be the most effective way to learn how to write SQL. As you become more accustomed to writing SQL, you will find that you begin to *think in SQL*. For me, when presented with a GIS conundrum, I constantly find myself thinking about the SQL solution, rather than the classical GIS commands.

SQL is very easy to understand query language, even for those who are unfamiliar with programming. When I began this book, I had no idea whether PostGIS could complete a majority of the tasks using only the SQL engine. I was quite pleased to see that virtually all of the tasks listed in *How do I do that in ArcGIS/Manifold* could actually be accomplished with the SQL engine in PostGIS. Also, I greatly enjoyed working through the MapAlgebra functionality and raster data analysis.

I welcome you to participate in the discussion of this book on my blog: **artlembo.wordpress.com**.

Arthur J. Lembo, Jr.
July, 2015

Table of Contents

How to understand this guide vi

Adding a column to a table 2

Sorting tabular or graphical data 3

Calculating values for new fields using arithmetic or related tables - making field calculations. 4

Relating data files and fields 5

Database Creation 7

Digitizing 8

Assigning Topology - identifying intersection points 9

Creating a Polygon from Line Segments (not illustrated) 10

Creating a distance buffer from line segments 11

Correcting topological errors - eliminating overlaps, undershoots, and dangles. (not illustrated) 12

Import and export - importing database tables, raster data, and vector data 13

Data Manipulation and Analysis 15

Vector Retrieval - Select by Window 16

Raster Retrieval - select data by area masks 17

Data restructuring - convert from raster to vector; and vector to raster 18

Modify raster cell size by resampling 18

Reducing unnecessary coordinates - weeding 19

Smoothing data to recover sinuosity (not illustrated) 19

Data restructuring - changing raster values by selected area or feature 20

Generate a TIN from point data 21

Kriging from point data (not illustrated) 22

Generate contour data from points (not illustrated) 22

Generate contour data from raster (not illustrated) 22

Data Transformation - mathematical transformation of raster data (not illustrated) 23

Projection definition and coordinate transformation 24

Vector overlay - polygon in polygon overlay; point in polygon overlay; line in polygon overlay 25

Raster processing - mathematical operations on one raster (sine, cosine, exponent) 26

Raster processing - mathematical operations on two rasters - adding, subtracting, minimum, maximum 27

Neighborhood functions - average, minimum, maximum, most frequent 28

Statistical functions - calculating areas, perimeters and lengths 31

Cross tabulation of two data categories 32

General - specify distance buffers; polygons within a distance of selected buffers; find nearest features 33

3D analysis - generating slope and aspect 34

Identifying watersheds 35

Network functions - choosing the optimal path through a network 35

Defining a drive-time zone 35

Geocoding addresses (not illustrated) 36

Topological intersection 37

    Intersect 37

    Union 38

    Identity 39

How to understand this guide

This guide follows the topic headings from the book *How do I do that in ArcGIS/Manifold*, as a way to illustrate the capabilities of PostGIS for accomplishing classic GIS tasks. You will notice that several gaps exist where the tasks cannot be completed using SQL, and would require the GUI. In some instances the gaps are logical as the specified task requires user interaction. In other cases, however, the gap exists because a function that one might assume would be a logical addition to the software simply was not built into the PostGIS SQL engine. A good example of this is the creation of area features from connected (spaghetti) lines.

All of the SQL queries were tested on a PostGRES dump file you can download from artlembo.wordpress.com. The SQL in PostGRES is ANSI compliant, and the functions in PostGIS conform to the Open Geospatial Consortium (OGC) specifications. Therefore, much of the SQL in this book can likely be used in other ANSI compliant databases that make use of the OGC specifications. All of the queries were written in the most straightforward way possible – however, as you learn SQL, you will discover other ways to accomplishing the tasks. In many cases, there may be more efficient ways to accomplish the task.

I have attempted to indent the queries as best as possible so that it is easier to read. However, there are some examples that have too long of names, or too much code to fit on a single line on the page. In these cases, there may be some minor *wrapping* of the text.

Database Management

Database management functions provide for tracking, retrieval, storage, update, protection, and archiving of stored data.

page 29. The Process for Selecting Geographic Information Systems

Adding a column to a table

Adding a column to a table is relatively straightforward in SQL. The original *How do I do that in ArcGIS/Manifold* document did not include options like changing the name, data type, or size of the columns. Nonetheless, the following shows a few examples on how to modify tables using the `ALTER TABLE` command in SQL.

To add a new column (in this case, a column named **HomeAge** that stores Integers, the user simply writes:

Add a column

```
ALTER TABLE parcels
ADD COLUMN homeage INTEGER
```

Rename a column

```
ALTER TABLE parcels
RENAME COLUMN homeage TO age_of_home
```

Alter the type

```
ALTER TABLE parcels
ALTER COLUMN propclass TYPE varchar

ALTER TABLE parcels
ALTER COLUMN propclass TYPE integer USING
trim(propclass)::integer
```

Remove a column

```
ALTER TABLE parcels
DROP COLUMN age_of_home
```

Sorting tabular or graphical data

Using SQL, we can sort the data on any field, combination of fields, or even an on-the-fly calculated field. Sorting can be done in either ascending or descending order.

<u>Sort in descending order</u>

```
SELECT parcelkey, asmt FROM parcels
ORDER BY asmt DESC
```

<u>Sort multiple fields</u>

```
SELECT parcelkey, acres, asmt, addrstreet FROM parcels
ORDER BY asmt, acres
```

<u>Sort using an on-the-fly calculation</u>[2]

```
SELECT parcelkey, (asmt - land) AS structurevalue
FROM parcels
ORDER BY structurevalue DESC
```

---

[2] when renaming a column from an SQL query, we typically use the AS directive. However, PostGRES does not require that you use AS – although its inclusion allows for easier reading.

Calculating values for new fields using arithmetic or related tables - making field calculations.

New values may be calculated using the UPDATE statement, or values can be calculated on-the-fly without changing the actual data in a table. You can calculate data as a result of an SQL SELECT query, or as a calculation into an existing field. Generally, calculating new values is performed using the UPDATE statement on a column for a table.

The following example updates a field named homevalue in our parcels table by subtracting the value of the land from the entire assessment value of the property:

```
UPDATE parcels
SET homevalue =  parcels.asmt - parcels.land
```

Calculations on a related table

You can also use a table relation, and update the value in one table with values in another table that are related by a common field. In this example we are subtracting the land value in the parvalues table from the asmt value in the parcels table. To accomplish this, the inner SELECT query performs a calculation on the fly, and also relates the parcel table to the parvalues table. This inner query is treated as a virtual table that is then used within the UPDATE statement:

```
UPDATE parcels
SET homevalue = parcels.asmt - parvalues.land
FROM parvalues
WHERE parcels.parcelkey = parvalues.parcelkey
```

Calculations without updating the table

The following performs a calculation on-the-fly to determine the tax amount for a property, based upon its assessed value as part of a SELECT query, without updating an existing field:

```
SELECT (parcels.asmt * .07) AS TaxValue
FROM parcels
```

Relating data files and fields

SQL relates can work on more than one table. This example illustrates how to relate multiple tables together based on a related item. While many complex relates are possible in SQL, simple tables are used here to illustrate the process. For example, we can join two tables (parcels and propclas) as:

```
SELECT parcels.parcelkey, parcels.propclass,propclas.description
FROM parcels, propclas
WHERE parcels.propclass = propclas.value
```

Unfortunately, the previous query will return an error because the *value* field in the propclas table is represented as a text value, while the *propclass* field in the parcels table is an Integer value. However, SQL can create the relationship by simply changing the data type of the *value* field on-the-fly to an Integer using the CAST operator:

```
SELECT parcels.parcelkey, parcels.propclass,propclas.description
FROM parcels, propclas
WHERE parcels.propclass = Cast(propclas.value as integer)
```

We can also join the tables on the left or right using the JOIN[3] statement:

```
SELECT parcels.parcelkey, parcels.propclass,
propclas.description
FROM parcels
RIGHT JOIN propclas
ON parcels.propclass = CAST(propclas.value as integer)
```

Right outer joins include all of the records from the second (right) of two tables, even if there are no matching values for records in the first (left) table.

```
SELECT parcels.parcelkey, parcels.propclass,
propclas.description
FROM parcels
LEFT JOIN propclas
ON parcels.propclass = CAST(propclas.value as integer)
```

Left outer joins include all of the records from the first (left) of two tables, even if there are no matching values for records in the second (right) table.

---

[3] The JOIN statement is ordinarily a faster method for joining data than the full scan approach shown previous to it.

Another option instead of using CAST, is to convert the value using the :: notation as:

```
SELECT parcels.parcelkey, parcels.propclass,
propclas.description
FROM parcels
LEFT JOIN propclas
ON parcels.propclass =  propclas.value :: integer
```

Database Creation

Database creation functions are those functions required to convert spatial data into a digital form that can be used by a GIS. This includes digitizing features found on printed maps or aerial photographs and transformation of existing digital data into the internal format of a given GIS.

Page 29, The Process for Selecting Geographic Information Systems

Digitizing

Ordinarily, digitizing is performed within the GUI of a GIS where the user points-and-clicks on the screen. However, sometimes SQL can be used if you have a table of coordinate values you want to enter in, or if you are receiving input from say an Internet based application. The following examples illustrate how to insert geometries into an existing layer.

Points are created from two coordinate values using the ST_MakePoint function. Those points must then be assigned a coordinate system (SRID) using the ST_SetSRID function as:

```
ST_SetSRID(ST_MakePoint(X,Y),SRID number))
```

In this example, we are inserting a point and an OID value into the "trees" table and assigning it to New York State Place Central Zone (2261):

```
INSERT into trees(geometry)
Values(ST_SetSRID(ST_MakePoint(833240,888478),2261));
```

If you had a table of X and Y values, you could insert all of them into a new layer as:

```
INSERT into trees (geometry)
SELECT ST_SetSRID(ST_MakePoint(easting, northing),2261)
FROM treetable
```

Lines are created from a series of point geometries. To add a Line, you could string together a series of ST_MakePoint functions. In the following example we are adding New York State Plane Central Zone (SRID 2261) points and converting them into a line using ST_MakeLine:

```
INSERT INTO hydro ("OID",geometry)
Values(50000,ST_SetSRID(ST_MakeLine(ST_MakePoint(808647,942424),
                    ST_MakePoint(853828, 889564)),2261))
```

Areas are created as a series of coordinates. While you can string together a series of points, the following example uses the Well Known Text (WKT) format to create a linestring and then the ST_MakePolygon function to convert the linestring to an area:

```
INSERT INTO parks ("OID",geometry)
Values(50001,ST_SetSRID(ST_MakePolygon
 (ST_GeomFromText('LINESTRING(849268 886123,808647 893424,897647
                    893424, 849268 886123)')),2261)
    )
```

Assigning Topology - identifying intersection points

You can find intersection points for either line or area geometries in a single layer as:

```
ST_Intersection(geometry, geometry)
```

<u>Intersections on a single layer</u>

```
SELECT ST_Intersection(roads.geometry,roads.geometry)
FROM roads
```

<u>Intersections on multiple layers</u>[4]

```
SELECT ST_Intersection(roads.geometry,hydro.geometry)
FROM roads, hydro
WHERE ST_Intersects(roads.geometry,hydro.geometry)
```

Also, you can insert the intersection points into a new layer using the `INSERT` command:

```
INSERT into scratchlayer (geometry)
 (SELECT ST_Intersection(roads.geometry,hydro.geometry)
   FROM roads, hydro
   WHERE ST_Intersects(roads.geometry,hydro.geometry)
   )
```

---

[4] Combining ST_Intersection with ST_Intersects accomplishes two things: it speeds up the query because intersection points are only created for those lines that intersect. Also, it reduces the number of *null* values returned because if you ask PostGIS to return the ST_Intersection of two lines that don't intersect, it will obey your wish: that is, it will return a null value.

Creating a Polygon from Line Segments (not illustrated)

Creating a polygon from multiple line segments (spaghetti) is not possible in PostGIS.

Creating a distance buffer from line segments

Buffers can be created on any type of geometry, either points, lines, or areas - using the Buffer statement as:

```
ST_Buffer(geometry,distance)
```

The units can be virtually any unit such as meters, feet, miles, kilometers, etc.

<u>Buffer with a constant value</u>

```
SELECT ST_buffer(geometry,50)
FROM hydro
```

<u>Buffer with an attribute assigned value</u>

```
SELECT ST_buffer(geometry,hydro.length)
FROM hydro
```

<u>Creating ringed buffers around a geometry</u>[5]:

```
SELECT name, ST_Buffer(geometry, 50) AS g
FROM parks

UNION ALL
SELECT name, ST_Buffer(geometry, 30) AS g
FROM parks

UNION ALL
SELECT name, ST_Buffer(geometry, 20) AS g
FROM parks
```

Another approach to a ringed buffer is to use the VALUES statement to return a virtual table of the three distances:

```
SELECT parks.name, column1, ST_Buffer(geometry,column1) as g
FROM parks, (VALUES (10),(20),(30)) AS DistBuf
```

---

[5] UNION ALL assumes that the table structure for each query is the same - therefore, you must have the same fields and field types.

Correcting topological errors - eliminating overlaps, undershoots, and dangles. (not illustrated)

PostGIS does not natively eliminate overlays, undershoots, and dangles.

Import and export - importing database tables, raster data, and vector data

Database Tables

You can import a database table into an empty table, or even append the data to an existing table using the COPY command. Assuming we have a comma delimited file named treetable.csv, you would enter:

```
COPY treetable FROM 'c:/temp/treetable.csv' DELIMITER ',' CSV;
```

Raster Data

The next section in this book makes extensive use of raster data. Working with raster data in PostGIS is relatively simple, as all rasters are treated as tables with a column named *rast*. Loading raster data into PostGIS requires a command line function called `raster2pgsql`. As an example, assume we have a USGS DEM in the c:\temp\ drive. The command to load the DEM into PostGIS in the UTM Zone 18 meters (SRID 26718) is:

```
raster2pgsql -I -e -F -C -Y -s 26718 c:/temp/dem.asc dem | psql -d hdi -U postgres
```

Export Vector Data

Exporting vector data is simply using the PostGRES COPY command, along with the ST_ASText function. For example, you can output a WKT ascii file from the parcels table as:

```
COPY (SELECT ST_AsText(geometry), parcel.parcelkey FROM parcels) TO 'c:/temp/parcels.csv' CSV HEADER;
```

PAGE INTENTIONALLY BLANK

Data Manipulation and Analysis

Data manipulation and analysis functions provide the capability to selectively retrieve, transform, restructure, and analyze data.

Retrieval options provide the ability to retrieve either graphic features or feature attributes in a variety of ways. Transformation includes both coordinate/projection transformations and coordinate adjustments. Data restructuring includes the ability to convert vector data to raster data, merge data, compress data, reclassify or rescale data, and contour, triangulate, or grid random or uniformly spaced z-value data sets

Analysis functions differ somewhat depending on whether the internal data structure is raster or vector based. Analysis functions provide the capability to create new maps and related descriptive statistics by reclassifying and combining existing data categories in a variety of ways. Analysis functions also support: replacement of cell values with neighboring cell characteristics (neighborhood analysis); defining distance buffers around points, lines and areas (proximity analysis); optimum path or route selection (network analysis); and generating slope, aspect and profile maps (terrain analysis).

Page 29, The Process for Selecting Geographic Information Systems.

Vector Retrieval - Select by Window

Although *select by window* normally assumes an interactive session with the GUI, you can use SQL to select by geometric shape. In this example, we are entering a WKT expression for a triangle. All vector features intersecting the box are selected. Instead of intersecting, the query could use contains or touches[6]:

```
SELECT parcels.*
FROM parcels,
   (VALUES (ST_SetSRID(ST_MakePolygon(ST_GeomFromText
            ('LINESTRING(849268 886123,808647 893424,897647 893424,
                         849268 886123)')),2261))
   ) AS g
WHERE ST_Intersects(geometry,column1)
```

In the above example, the polygon is simply a triangle. You could easily add more points to create a more detailed polygon, or you could create a rectangle.

---

[6] The VALUES statement returns a table, with a column named Column1.

Raster Retrieval - select data by area masks

We can select raster pixels using the ST_Clip function. ST_Clip works on vectors as well as rasters. In this case, instead of passing ST_CLIP two vector objects, we pass it a set of raster pixels from the DEM layer (dem.rast), and a geometry from the waterway layer. Returning the resulting clip with the name `rast` will allow GIS products such as QGIS to understand the layer to be a raster. Using the INTO statement, we can easily write the results into a new raster table:

```
SELECT ST_Clip(dem.rast,geometry,true) AS rast
INTO waterdem1
FROM waterway, dem
```

You ca also create a polygon on the fly like our earlier example and clip out the raster:

```
SELECT ST_Clip(dem.rast,column1,true) AS rast
INTO waterdem2
FROM dem, (VALUES (ST_SetSRID(ST_MakePolygon
        (ST_GeomFromText('LINESTRING(380000 4697300,381000
        4697300,381000 4699300, 380000 4697300)')),26718))) AS
        g
```

Data restructuring - convert from raster to vector; and vector to raster

Raster to Vector

PostGIS can convert a raster layer to vector using the ST_Polygon function as:

```
SELECT ST_Polygon(rast)
INTO parkvec
FROM parkras
```

Vector to Raster

You can also convert a vector file to raster format using the ST_Raster function as:

```
SELECT
ST_AsRaster(geometry,dem.rast) AS rast
INTO parkrast
FROM parks,dem
```

Modify raster cell size by resampling

There are a number of ways to modify a raster cell. The following example rescales the DEM from 10m grid cells to 100m grid cells:

```
SELECT
ST_Rescale((rast),100) AS rast
INTO rastscale
FROM dem
```

Reducing unnecessary coordinates - weeding

You can simplify a geometry using the Douglas-Peucker algorithm using the ST_Simplify[7] functions as:

```
SELECT ST_Simplify(geometry,30)
INTO hydrosimp
FROM hydro
```

Smoothing data to recover sinuosity (not illustrated)

Smoothing data in PostGIS is currently not supported.

---

[7] PostGIS also has a function named ST_SimplifyPreserveTopology that will use the weeding algorithm but maintain the topological connectivity among shared lines.

Data restructuring - changing raster values by selected area or feature

Raster data can be altered where they intersect features in another layer with the ST_SetValue function as:

```
ST_SetValue(raster, geometry or raster,new value)
```

The features in the other layer can be either raster or vector. In this example we are combining a few different operations, namely, converting a raster data to a polygon, to show the flexibility offered.

```
SELECT ST_Setvalue(dem.rast,ST_Polygon(parkras.rast),3000) AS rast
INTO newrast
FROM dem, parkras
```

Generate a TIN from point data

Using a set of points, we can generate Triangulated Irregular Networks (TIN) using the ST_DelaunayTriangles function. In order to do that, all of the point geometries need to be joined together with the ST_Union function, and the resulting GeometryCollection returned from ST_DalaunayTriangles need to be extracted with ST_CollectionExtract. An example is:

```
SELECT
ST_CollectionExtract(ST_DelaunayTriangles(ST_Union(geometry)),2)
AS geometry
INTO tindraw
FROM elevpts
```

Kriging from point data (not illustrated)

Kriging is not performed in PostGIS.

Generate contour data from points (not illustrated)

PostGIS does not create contours from points.

Generate contour data from raster (not illustrated)

PostGIS does not create contours from a raster file.

Data Transformation - mathematical transformation of raster data (not illustrated)

Although PostGIS does allow rotation, translation, and scaling of raster, there isn't a function that would allow users to enter X,Y pairs for ground control and map units to determine the least squares transformation.

Projection definition and coordinate transformation

Geometries may be projected and defined on-the-fly with SQL in PostGIS. The following query projects the geometry from the parcels layer stored as *State Plane, NY Central* to the *UTM Zone 18* coordinate system obtained from the [dem] layer.

Change Projection

```
SELECT ST_Transform(geometry,3450)
FROM parcels;
```

Define Projection

If the geometry is in the correct numerical format, but does not have a coordinate system assigned, you can assign a coordinate system. For example, assume that the parcel layer does not have a coordinate system defined, but should actually be UTM 18N. The query would be:

```
SELECT UpdateGeometrySRID('elevpts','geometry',3450)
```

Vector overlay - polygon in polygon overlay; point in polygon overlay; line in polygon overlay

Overlaying and finding geometry features contained within polygons are the same whether using points, lines, or polygons, and would take the form of:

```
SELECT parcels.*
FROM parcels, parks
WHERE ST_Intersects(parks.geometry,parcels.geometry)
```

in this case, it does not matter whether the parcels are points, lines, or polygons. In addition to `ST_Intersects`, other operations may be used and include `ST_Touches`, `ST_Contains`, or `ST_Overlaps`.

Raster processing - mathematical operations on one raster (sine, cosine, exponent)

PostGIS has implemented an extensive Map Algebra library using the ST_MapAlgebra function. ST_MapAlgebra function requires four parameters: the rast field of the DEM, the band number, the pixel type, and then the map algebra function in quotes, with the raster value field (rast.val) in brackets ([ ]). Therefore, individual pixel values can be updated with a mathematical function as:

```
ST_MapAlgebra(raster field (rast),band number,pixel type,'map
algebra function')
```

Sine

```
SELECT ST_MapAlgebra(dem.rast,1,NULL,'(sin([rast1.val])*100)')
AS rast
INTO parkalg
FROM dem
```

Cosine

```
SELECT ST_MapAlgebra(dem.rast,1,NULL,'(cos([rast1.val])*100)')
AS rast
INTO parkalg
FROM dem
```

Exponent

```
SELECT ST_MapAlgebra(dem.rast,1,NULL,'(([rast1.val])^2)') AS
rast
INTO parkalg
FROM dem
```

Raster processing - mathematical operations on two rasters - adding, subtracting, minimum, maximum

PostGIS has extensive map algebra functions that can work on two rasters. Similar to the single raster version, the input to the ST_MapAlgebra function are the raster field of the first raster (called [rast1], the raster field of the second raster layer ([rast2], and the map algebra function.

Addition

```
SELECT ST_MapAlgebra(dem.rast,rasslope.rast,
       ('[rast1] + [rast2]')) AS rast
INTO rasalgb
FROM dem, rasslope
```

Subtraction

```
SELECT ST_MapAlgebra(dem.rast,rasslope.rast,
       ('[rast1] - [rast2]')) AS rast
INTO rasalgb
FROM dem, rasslope
```

Multiplicationn

```
SELECT ST_MapAlgebra(dem.rast,rasslope.rast,
       ('[rast1] * [rast2]')) AS rast
INTO rasalgb
FROM dem, rasslope
```

Neighborhood functions - average, minimum, maximum, most frequent

The ST_MapAlgebra functions have a number of built in functions that allow you to compute average, minimum, and maximum among others within a neighborhood of cells, as shown below. With a little more effort, you can create a function to perform the same analysis using SQL embedded in the MapAlgebra call (please see note on functions at the end of this section).

<u>Minimum</u>

```
SELECT
 ST_MapAlgebra (rast, 1,'ST_Min4ma(double precision[][][],
                integer[][],text[])'::regprocedure,'32BF',
                'FIRST', NULL, 1, 1
                ) AS rast
INTO minrast
FROM dem;
```

<u>Sum</u>

```
SELECT
 ST_MapAlgebra (rast, 1,'ST_Sum4ma(double precision[][][],
                integer[][],text[])'::regprocedure,'32BF',
                'FIRST',NULL, 1, 1
                ) AS rast
INTO sumrast
FROM dem;
```

<u>Maximum</u>

```
SELECT
 ST_MapAlgebra (rast, 1,'ST_Max4ma(double precision[][][],
                integer[][],text[])'::regprocedure,'32BF',
                'FIRST',NULL, 1, 1
                ) AS rast
INTO maxrast
FROM dem;
```

Mean

```
SELECT
  ST_MapAlgebra (rast, 1,'ST_Mean4ma(double precision[][][],
                integer[][],text[])'::regprocedure,'32BF',
                'FIRST',NULL, 1, 1
                ) AS rast
INTO maxrast
FROM dem;
```

A note on Functions

Neighborhood functions can also be run using the MapAlgebra function with virtually any SQL statement. However, to accomplish neighborhood functions, you must create a function that the ST_MapAlgebra references. Although a little trickier to write, the flexibility of using SQL syntax is well worth the effort. The following query creates a Function named Sql_MapAlbebra.

```
CREATE or REPLACE FUNCTION
   SQL_MapAlgebra(value float8[][][], pos integer[][][], VARIADIC
                userargs text[] DEFAULT NULL::text[]
                )
RETURNS double precision AS
 $$
   SELECT min(p) :: double precision FROM unnest($1) As p;
 $$
LANGUAGE sql IMMUTABLE;

SELECT
  ST_MapAlgebra (rast, 1,
                'SQL_MapAlgebra(double precision[][][],
                integer[][], text[])'::regprocedure,
                '8BUI', 'FIRST', NULL, 1, 1
                ) AS rast
INTO maxrast
FROM dem;
```

The bold portion of the query is where the actual SQL function is initiated. Also, the bold italics *1,1* define the kernel window used for the search. Using a window of 1,1 will evaluate pixels on either side of the center pixel, or in this case a 3x3 window, while using *2,2* will create a 5,5 window. You can replace the **boldface** portion with any other SQL query.

The following query verifies the number of pixels used in the kernel with the COUNT function.

```
SELECT count(p) :: double precision FROM unnest($1) As p;
```

Selecting the most frequent value (often called majority) can be obtained by a SELECT query that determines the COUNT of all the values in the kernel window, sorts the result by the count in descending order, and then obtains the first record using the LIMIT 1 statement (due to the sort in descending order, the first record is the most frequent value):

```
SELECT cnt :: double precision v FROM
     (SELECT count(v) cnt, (p) :: double precision
      FROM unnest($1) As p
      GROUP BY p
      ORDER by cnt DESC LIMIT 1
     ) AS p;
```

Statistical functions - calculating areas, perimeters and lengths

Descriptive statistics on geometries can be calculated to include area, length, or perimeter. In the example below, "parks" are an area feature so to obtain the length, we are extracting the boundary from the area.

```
SELECT ST_Area(geometry) AS area,
       ST_Length(ST_Boundary(geometry)) AS perimeter
FROM parks
```

Cross tabulation of two data categories

Cross tabulation matrices are created by using the TRANSFORM function in conjunction with a PIVOT table. In this example, we are summing the area of each park (parks) that intersects a flood polygon (firm]), and cross tabulating it with the actual flood zone. Also, the small calculation in the first line returns the area in square feet, and then divides that by 43,560 to convert the area to acres. Unfortunately, the flood zones need to be manually entered (`sumarea text, A text, X text, AE text, X500 text`).

```
SELECT *
FROM Crosstab
  ('SELECT  "name" :: text,"zone" :: text,
    Sum(ST_Area(ST_intersection
                        (parks.geometry,firm.geometry))/43560)
                        :: text AS sumArea
   FROM parks, firm
   WHERE ST_Intersects(parks.geometry,firm.geometry)
   GROUP BY "name","zone"
   ORDER BY 1,2 '
  ) AS ct
(sumarea text, A text, X text, AE text, X500 text)
```

General - specify distance buffers; polygons within a distance of selected buffers; find nearest features

The ability to specify distance buffers was already addressed in a previous section. However, finding polygons within a specified distance and finding nearest features are calculated as:

Polygons within a distance

```
SELECT parcels.*
FROM parcels, parks
WHERE ST_Distance(parcels.geometry,parks.geometry) < 500
```

Nearest Features

Selecting the nearest features in PostGIS is actually trickier due to PostGRES not having a `First` aggregate clause. Therefore, to find the nearest feature, you must first calculate the distance between all the features in both layers. After that calculation (shown as `mindist` in the subquery below), you must create another virtual table of all the distances between the layers and perform a `LEFT JOIN` on the second layer where the calculated distance between the two layers is the same as the minimum distance for the first layer. This query finds the closest park from each tree - however, to speed the query up, a distance threshold of 200 ft. is used as a cutoff value.

```
SELECT site_id, park_no, minium_distance
FROM
  (SELECT min(dist) AS minium_distance,site_id
   FROM (SELECT parks.park_no, trees.site_id,
         st_distance(parks.geometry, trees.geometry) AS dist
         FROM parks, trees
         WHERE st_distance(parks.geometry,trees.geometry) < 200
         ORDER BY dist, park_no
        ) AS mindist
  GROUP BY site_id
  ) AS T
LEFT JOIN (SELECT park_no, site_id s_id,
           st_distance(parks.geometry, trees.geometry) AS dd
           FROM parks, trees) AS T2
ON
   site_id = s_id AND dd = minium_distance
```

3D analysis - generating slope and aspect

Slope and aspect require a raster layer and a location for where the user wants the slope and height to calculated. The location is returned as a point geometry.

<u>Slope</u>

```
SELECT ST_Slope(rast) AS rast
INTO
rasslope
FROM dem
```

<u>Aspect</u>

```
SELECT ST_Aspect(rast) AS rast
INTO
rasslope
FROM dem
```

Identifying watersheds

PostGIS does not support the creation of watersheds.

Network functions - choosing the optimal path through a network

Network functions are supported through an add-in product called pg_Routing. Pg_Routing is an extensive routing engine, and beyond the scope of this book.

Defining a drive-time zone

Network functions are supported through an add-in product called pg_Routing. Pg_Routing is an extensive routing engine, and beyond the scope of this book.

Geocoding addresses (not illustrated)

PostGIS performs geocoding through the TIGER geocoding module which is beyond the scope of this book.

Topological intersection[8]

SQL in PostGIS supports all of the classical topological intersection methods (intersect, union, identity) using variations of the ST_Intersection and st_Difference methods. These capabilities are more sophisticated than most SQL presented in this book. Nonetheless, the command builds upon the more foundational SQL that you have already seen. The parcel and parks layers are used as illustrative examples:

Intersect

The basic principle for intersection is to clip two area layers using the ClipIntersect function, and then joining the subsequent data tables to the clipped features.

```
SELECT * FROM
    (SELECT parcels."OID" paoid, parks."OID" AS poid,
            st_intersection(parks.geometry,parcels.geometry)
     FROM parks, parcels
     WHERE st_intersects(parks.geometry,parcels.geometry)
    ) AS a
RIGHT JOIN parks on poid = parks."OID"
RIGHT JOIN parcels on paoid = parcels."OID"
```

---

[8] for these examples, we are using the id field to obtain the geometry rather than the [geom (i)] field so as to provide less clutter on the page.

Union

Union is slightly more complicated and requires the joining of three separate queries: clipping the two layers together with ST_Intersection, obtaining the parts of layer 1 that are not in layer 2 using ST_Difference, and obtaining the parts of layer 2 that are not in layer 1. After the geometries are assembled, the attribute tables are joined in. In this example we will overlay the firm layer and the parks layer:

```
SELECT * FROM
(
  SELECT
  ST_Intersection(firm.geometry,parks.geometry) g,
              firm."OID" :: integer AS cid,
              parks."OID" :: integer AS rid
  FROM firm, parks
  WHERE ST_Intersects(firm.geometry,parks.geometry)

 UNION ALL

  SELECT
  ST_Difference(parks.geometry,firm.geometry) AS g,
              firm."OID" :: integer AS cid,
              parks."OID" :: integer AS rid
  FROM firm, parks

UNION ALL

  SELECT
  ST_Difference(firm.geometry,parks.geometry) AS g,
              firm."OID" :: integer AS cid,
              parks."OID" :: integer AS rid
  FROM firm, parks

) AS a

RIGHT JOIN firm ON firm."OID" = cid
RIGHT JOIN parks ON parks."OID" = rid
```

Identity

```sql
SELECT * FROM
(
 SELECT
   ST_Intersection(firm.geometry,parks.geometry) g,
               firm."OID" :: integer AS cid,
               parks."OID" :: integer AS rid
   FROM firm, parks
   WHERE ST_Intersects(firm.geometry,parks.geometry)

   UNION ALL

   SELECT
   ST_Difference(parks.geometry,firm.geometry) AS g,
               firm."OID" :: integer AS cid,
               parks."OID" :: integer AS rid
   FROM firm, parks
   WHERE ST_Intersects(firm.geometry,parks.geometry)
) AS a

RIGHT JOIN firm ON firm."OID" = cid
RIGHT JOIN parks ON parks."OID" = rid
```

Made in the USA
Middletown, DE
29 June 2015